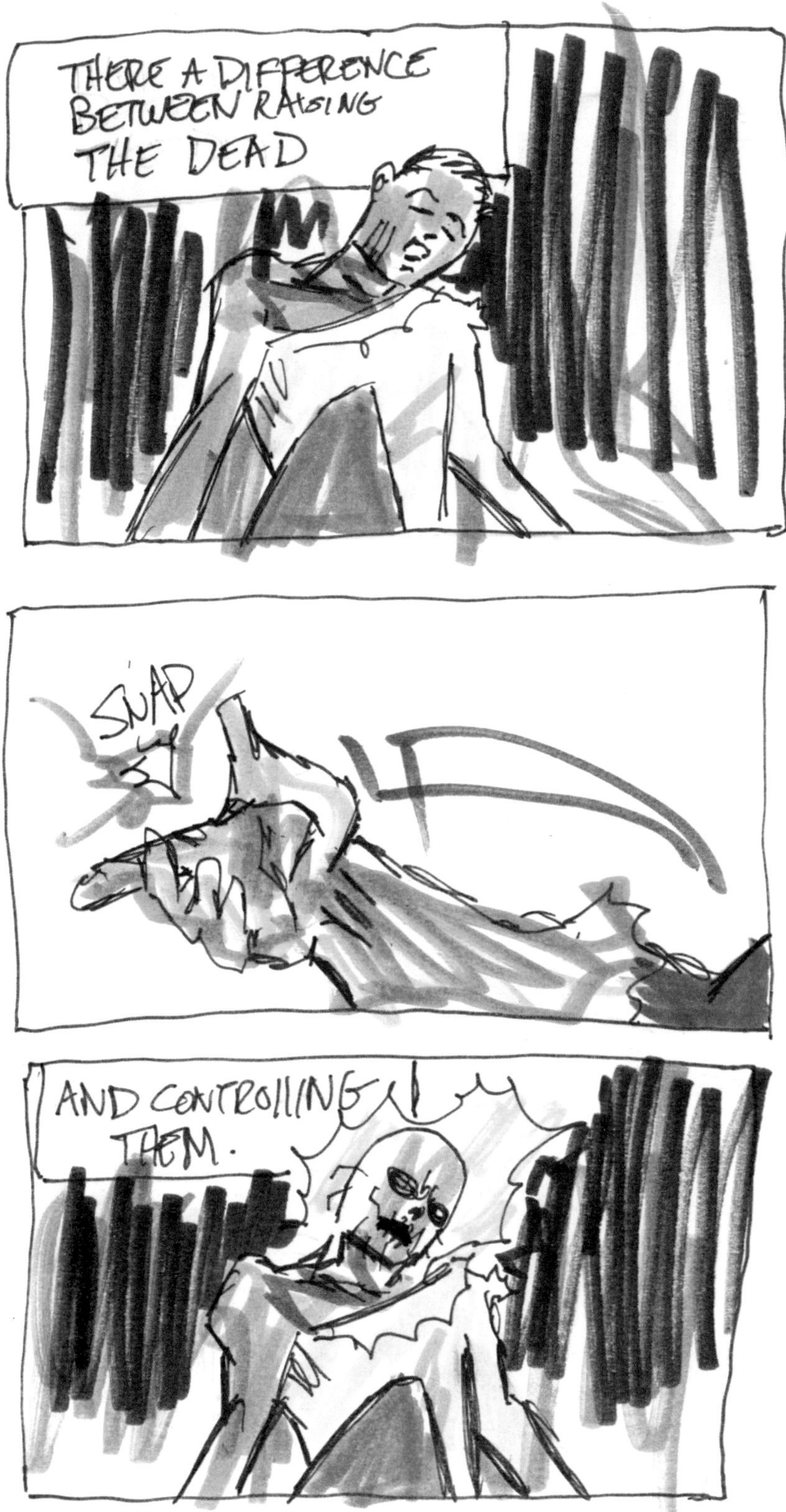
THERE A DIFFERENCE BETWEEN RAISING THE DEAD
SNAP
AND CONTROLLING THEM.

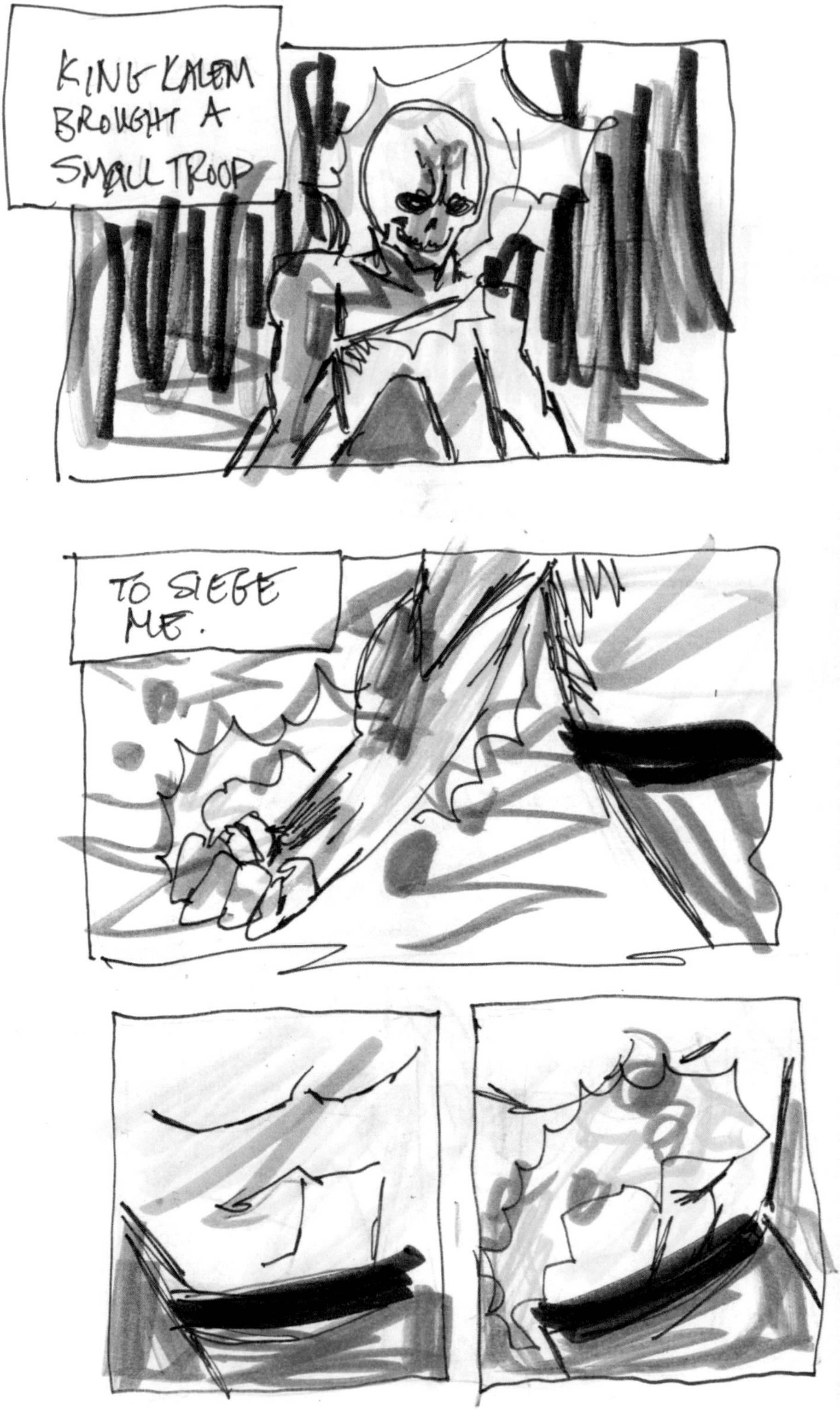
KING KALEM BROUGHT A SMALL TROOP
TO SIEGE ME.

SUFFICE TO SAY...

DIDN'T WORK.

NOW, THEY ARE MY ARMY...

SO SAYS...

KR'UL
AH! BEING EVIL IS SO FUN!
HIS VOICE, BIONIC AND HOLLOW. GESTURING FLAMBOYANTLY HE CONTINUES...

BRING FORTH KING KALEM!

KR'UL!
LEAVE MY ARMY TO REST IN PEACE.
THEY WEREN'T ALWAYS DEAD YOU KNOW!

NOTHING MORE THAN. A SHEEPISHLY GUISED SKELETON, GLOWING OF PSIONIC ENERGY.
WHY HAVE YOU COME TO ME?!
A WARLOK, KR'UL, USES HIS ABILITY FOR HIS OWN TWISTED WAYS.

YOU HAVE ANOTHER PRISONER HERE.
OH !?

...THE GIRL.

I ALWAYS CONSIDERED LOVE TO BE-- A WEAKNESS!

EVERY ONE LOVES SOME ONE... SOME THING.
...

WHERE IS SHE?

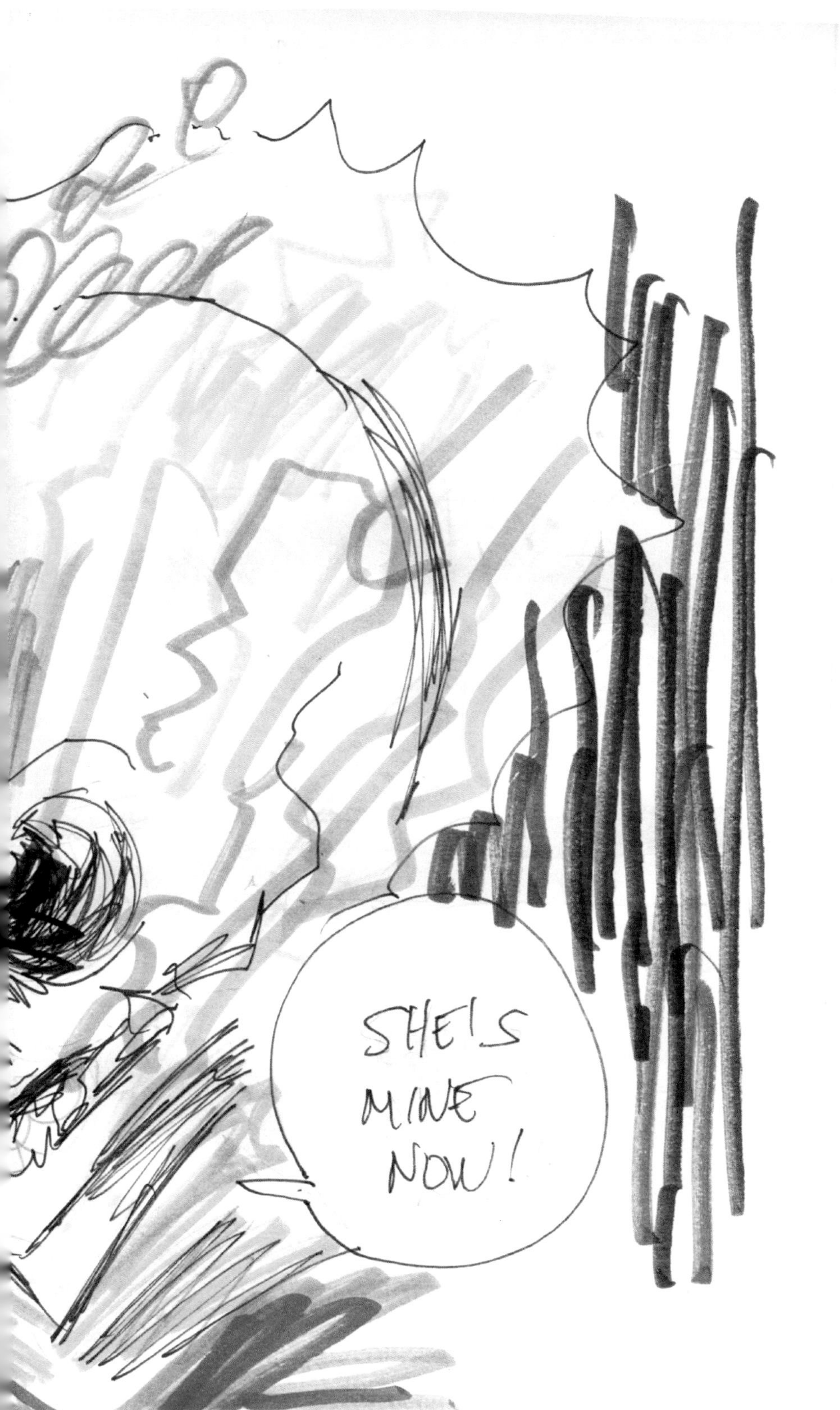
SHE'S MINE NOW!

LOCK HIM UP!
AND BRING HER TO ME!

LATER.
ENTER SA THE EPIPHANY.
IN SHACKLES AND CHAINS AND WEARY FROM BATTLE.
YOU'RE ATTEMPT TO SHUT ME DOWN FAILED, MS EPIPHANY!
EVEN IN EXILE YOU WISH TO BE A HERO.
AND FAILED.

I AM OFFERING YOU HOPE, POWER, AND TO BE MY QUEEN!

?

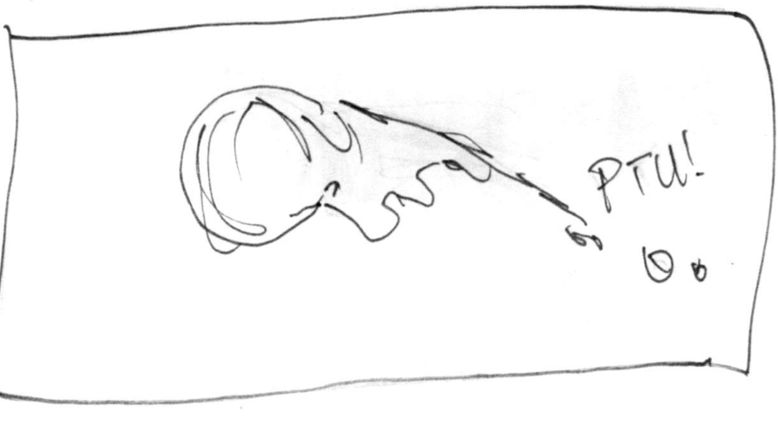
PTU!

GET HER OUT OF HERE!
I'LL GIVE YOU SOME TIME TO RECONSIDER.

LOCK HER UP TOO!!!

GET IN THERE

SA!
TO BE CONTINUED...

9 781006 601484

Lightning Source UK Ltd.
Milton Keynes UK
UKRC012345060921
390147UK00007B/111/J